Daniel T. Darmody

HOW TO LIVE
WITH A VIRGO:
A SURVIVAL GUIDE

Illustrations by
LILY AMIRPOUR

 www.trafford.com

North America & international
toll-free: 1 888 232 4444 (USA & Canada)
fax: 812 355 4082

Dedications

For my wife, Jean,
without whom I wouldn't have
had the need to write this book.

And for my parents,
my wonderful mother, Pearline,
and my dearly departed father, John,
who always told me I could accomplish
anything I set my mind to.

Contents

Acknowledgments

I'd like to thank all of the Virgos in my life whose eccentricities have contributed to this work, including my wife's brother, our grandchildren, clients, and all of our Virgo acquaintances.

Heartfelt thanks to Lily Amirpour for bringing my concepts to life in her illustrations throughout this book. Kudos to Lily for "getting" it.

Lastly, thanks to my wife, Jean Headley Darmody, "Clean Jean the Typing Queen," for her technical expertise in the proofreading and editing of this book, and also for being "The Virgo" in my life.

Preface

Let me preface this book by saying that I have not acquired all of my knowledge of Virgos from books or newspaper horoscopes. No, I did it the hard way, by actually marrying one! Our marriage is a happy one, but not without considerable patience on my part. Admittedly, I am not the easiest person in the world to live with either, being an Aquarius, but that is for another book. I do not write this book to make fun of or pick on Virgos, but at the urging of my wife and other couples, where one of the two is a Virgo. The assertions that I have made have never been met with anger, but rather with knowing laughter! So, please don't hate me for stating what I see as the truth. Instead, read on and laugh with us at the many ways in which Virgos affect our lives, whether we realize it or not. You just may find that Virgos will grow on you. And please, if you are a Virgo or an astrologer and you see something that doesn't ring true, be aware that I do not write this book as a Virgo or an astrologer, but rather as someone whose life is affected daily by Virgos (I know many!).

The Zodiac:

AN ILLUSION YOU MUST LIVE WITH

The zodiac is an imaginary swath of the sky along which the stars, Sun, Moon, and planets appear to move. The zodiac is roughly 18 degrees in width and is tilted at an angle of 33.5 degrees relative to the equator. This swath is also the parade ground for twelve constellations listed by Ptolemy in Star Catalogue of AD 150 as Aries the Ram, Taurus the Bull, Gemini the Twins, Cancer the Crab, Leo the Lion, Virgo the Virgin, Libra the Scales (the only inanimate sign), Scorpius the Scorpion, Sagittarius the Archer, Capricorn the Goat, Aquarius the Water Carrier, and Pisces the Fish. There are other constellations, too—Orphiuchus, bits of Cetus, Sextants, and Orion—but for most purposes they are ignored.

Astroworld–All India On-Line

http://www.aiol.com/horoscope/zodiac.htm

VIRGO

Virgo is the sixth Sign of the Zodiac. The first five Signs represent the growth of the individual, and Virgos bring their skills and talents together for the good of others. Virgo is the Sign of Service. Despite their inherent modesty, people born under Virgo are industrious and efficient when working for a good cause. They are neat and well organized. As the sixth Sign, Virgo also rules the sixth House: the House of Health.

Kelli Fox, Astrology.Net

Index of Rules

Introduction

Anyone who has lived with, worked with, or is acquainted with a Virgo knows why a survival guide could be an essential tool. Virgos are a unique breed, being one of the most recognizable signs of the zodiac. Whether you believe in horoscopes or not is really irrelevant when dealing with a Virgo, perhaps even to the extent of proving how close horoscopes can actually be to the truth. People with other signs can be recognizable, but never with the accuracy with which a Virgo can be recognized. I have rarely been wrong when I have stated that someone must be a Virgo after meeting them or hearing about something they did. Virgos are just that predictable.

Virgos also seem to be everywhere, which should make this book extremely popular. I commented to my wife that we sure do know a lot of Virgos, and she replied that maybe it is because so many people are partying and having fun during Christmas and New Year's that nine months later Voila! Another group of Virgos hits the planet with a vengeance. Although I have no empirical data on the subject to draw from, I would not be surprised if Virgo is the most heavily populated sign on earth (at least in the western world.) On a recent trip to Santa Catalina Island, California to celebrate my wife's and a good friend's birthday (they were born on the same day and year, two hundred miles from each other), we ran into so many Virgos it was truly amazing. We had gone there for their birthday and apparently so had a great deal of other Virgos. At dinner on their birthday we saw at least six other Virgo birthday parties. A couple next to us was a Virgo and Aquarius mating. We found this very interesting, since my wife and I and our two friends are the same combinations. Even our waitress was a Virgo! Although I can't say that there are actually more Virgos, there does seem to be some proof that there are. I believe that there may be as many as one out of five or one out of four among us that are Virgos.

Recently, we found my wife's son whom she had reluctantly given up for adoption at birth in 1967 and regretted it ever since. We discovered that we have four wonderful grandchildren. What do you suppose the odds of any of them being Virgos would be? Well, believe it or not, two of the four children are Virgos. Add to this that my wife's brother is a Virgo, she has several clients who are Virgos, and many of our friends are Virgos, and you begin to see why I believe that Virgos are everywhere!

Let me add that there are many different degrees of Virgoism. A Virgo born on the cusp is less likely to display as many of the Virgo traits as is someone born in the middle of Virgo. There are also a whole slew of rising signs, moons in Virgo, and other astrological calculations that I admit to being fairly ignorant about. I do know that someone of an entirely different sign could have Virgo rising in his or her house and display Virgoish traits, of which I am an example. It is possible to not even be a Virgo and find yourself with some of these same traits.

It is also possible to mistake a psychological handicap as being Virgo when, in fact, the person is what Freud called an anal-retentive. Freud theorized that someone whose growth was stifled at the stage of potty training could become fixated. This fixation with trying to control their bowel movements could lead to a personality that was always trying to control their environment. Such a person would also want everything in their world to have order and for that order to be under their control. Although Freud's theories were related to very sick individuals he was treating, I believe that many a so-called "normal" person can display varying degrees of fixation.

The point to all this is that there is a striking similarity to some Virgos and some anal-retentives. (I suppose it is possible that all of Freud's patients were Virgos, but this would invalidate a lot of his data; so let's just assume that his patients all had different astrological signs.) This means when you meet someone who fits the descriptions in this book, it might be necessary to ask them if he or she is a Virgo before applying these techniques. Although some of these techniques may work when dealing with an anal-retentive personality, I have not tested them. Use them in such cases at your own risk. Enjoy!

Chapter One

VIRGOS ARE PERFECT

Rule One: <u>**Virgos are perfect!**</u> All other rules are based on this very simple statement. The Virgo is a perfectionist. Let me repeat this, because this is perhaps the single most important piece of information in this book. The Virgo is a perfectionist. This is so important to understand if you want to delve into the depths of what makes a Virgo tick.

I know this to be true for so many reasons. My wife is never wrong. Although she will sometimes give up the fight and say I am right, I know that *she* doesn't believe it. Even when there is irrefutable evidence that I am right, she will only admit it reluctantly. One of the first survival techniques is to simply agree with a Virgo. This will save you a lot of time, frustration, and antacid. You may very well be an expert in the field and know that you are right, but your best defense is to just admit that you are wrong. Virgos **really** like that. It may also earn you points for future redemption in other disputes. Earn enough points and you may just get your favorite Virgo to admit that you are right about something. Of course, extra points are awarded if an alternate expert proves you right. Beware that when you prove a Virgo to be wrong, you will upset them. The upset that is created may be misconstrued as being an upset about something else, such as one of your traits that irritate them, but rest assured that they are really upset about being proven wrong.

For example, my wife is fond of naming actors during movies and she is often wrong (don't tell **her** that I said that). Once she insisted that an actress was Sandy Dennis and it turned out that it was some other actress entirely. If I try to convince her that she is wrong, I will miss half of the movie, so I have learned to say, "Let's look in the credits!" which saves a lot of trouble. Credits work well as an alternate expert. Credits are proof that even a Virgo will admit is undeniable. I've earned enough points with movie credits to be able to use my favorite line with my wife when she names an actor: "No, it's Sandy Dennis!" I say. She *loves* that.

The Virgo trait of believing that they are right makes them ideal candidates for championing causes. They will fight for a cause until they feel the odds are too strong for even them. If they lose, they will still believe that they were right and let other people know that *they* were wrong for years. The Virgo will rarely lose, though. They are tenacious fighters because it is in their nature to be right. This trait makes Virgos good at a great deal of things. (Yes, I am complimenting the Virgo for their rightness, therefore admitting that they are often right and earning valuable points.) If you need someone to head a committee, plan a party, or run for office, then there is no better choice than a Virgo (if you agree with them). My wife was the chairperson for the Fog Fest Parade Committee for many years (our community's yearly festival parade), a member of the former Fog Fest Board, recently the paid coordinator for FFOG (the new Fog Fest organizing committee), a board member of the Pacifica Chamber of Commerce, past treasurer of our local TOPS (Take Off Pounds Sensibly)

chapter, as well as running her own successful sec-
retarial service and handling the accounts for my
business. Not only does she do a brilliant job at all
these tasks, but she also loves every minute of it!
On top of all this, she plans all of our social events
and trips, keeps all of our checkbooks perfectly
balanced, juggles our finances to pay our bills, and
jumps to the aid of friends (and sometimes strang-
ers) in need. Although she gives up sleep and free
time to do all these things and occasionally com-
plains that she is too busy, I know that she loves it.
Give her another issue that she believes in and she
would be right there in the forefront leading the
charge! One of my favorite sayings of hers is, "In a
perfect world, I wouldn't have to worry about any
of this!" The funny thing is that she really thinks
the world should be perfect. She is not alone. All
of the Virgos whom I have interviewed or with
whom I have personal experience have similar
perfectionist tendencies. Whether it's how they
approach schoolwork, cleaning the house, or how
they present themselves, perfectionism is present.
Rule Number One: <u>Virgos are perfect!</u>

**Rule Number Two: <u>Never ask a Virgo to
prove themselves after they have done exceptional work.</u>** When our town's annual festival,
the Fog Fest, was in danger of disappearing after

fifteen years because the former committee was quitting, my wife put on her cape with the big "V" on it and decided to carry the torch. Using her super Virgo powers, she single-handedly refused to allow it to die. She met with the Chamber of Commerce and City officials, called on friends including four former mayors of Pacifica, and put together a group of people to fight to save the Fog Fest. After months of battling, they won the war and saved our local festival. When the new board was created, they invited Jean to be the paid coordinator since she had served on most of the committees over the years and knew what had to be done. She gladly took it on. Our home (which also houses Headley Office Services, my wife's typing, notary, and process serving business) became "Fog Fest Central." From March until October, my wife's office phone (which has extensions all over our house) began ringing at 7:00 a.m. and didn't quit ringing until after midnight. She often worked until 3:00 a.m. to get things done. She had committees for everything and hundreds of volunteers, but she did a tremendous amount herself because no one had the attention to detail that she has or knew the functions of many of the committees. She literally attended every committee meeting, sometimes two or three a day, and helped run most of them.

The festival turned out to be the most successful one ever. Due to the enormous amount of time she spent on Fog Fest that year, our personal finances took a big hit, but the Fog Fest was a huge success.

After all of this, it might be logical that they would ask her to do it the following year without question, but they requested her to write a job description. This might seem like a reasonable request, but I was right in the middle of the war zone and I know this would have been a mammoth task in itself, which she would not get paid for doing. They wanted to see what it is she does to see if it is worth what they pay her. This was a major mistake, because she is able to make three times the money promoting her own business with a lot less work. I encouraged her to quit and do her own thing, but it just isn't that simple. She loves the Fog Fest and worked on it with such emotion that it tore her apart that they wanted her to prove herself. This is akin to a slap in the face to a Virgo, who would be likely to get angry and quit. Even before they requested the job description, she wanted more money to continue because of the amount of time it took and the toll it took on our personal finances, but they wanted to pay her less. I feared that she would not continue the following year because of a few naysayers, but it turned out there were far more people who knew her true worth than there were those against her. Without her writing a job description, they offered her a new contract for the same money, but with a lot less work. She got what she wanted but then quit anyway when we found her son she had given up for adoption because she needed time for our new family. After she left the Fog Fest Board, they found out how much she did the hard way. The Fog Fest is still going on, but some important Fog Fest traditions have been lost. They really lost her because they were insisting she prove herself, even after the tremendous success of the previous festival. I believe she would have found a way to do it all if they hadn't asked her to prove herself. **Rule Number Two: <u>Never ask a Virgo to prove themself after they have done exceptional work.</u>**

Of course, the perfectionist nature of the Virgo makes them wonderful editors, because they *know* they will find mistakes. My wife edits all my writings and I challenge any professional editor to find any typos after she is done with it. She has even found mistakes after several people have edited something, certain that they had corrected everything, only to find their folly after she gives it back to them with new corrections made. One of her clients valiantly tries to give her documents for proofreading that have no mistakes, but he has not been able to get one past her yet without her finding more errors. She has edited my book so many times that it can even drive me crazy, even when I know she is right, but I have learned that to dispute her findings is usually folly. One time she even found an error in a published spelling dictionary in which a word was placed alphabetically wrong.

There are, to be sure, negative aspects to the Virgo perfectionism. The Virgo believes that things have their rightful place in the universe. I would bet that the often used quote, "A place for everything and everything in its place," was written by a Virgo. Every dish, spoon, or food item in our kitchen has a proper place and woe to the person who puts something away wrong. I let my wife decide where things belong in most cases, then try to follow the template that she lays out for me. Of course, I fail, at times, no matter how hard I try. Lucky for me that I am an Aquarius with Virgo rising and have spent years of study with Zen-like groups or I would be continually frustrated. Virgos can be downright nitpickers when it comes to things in the wrong place. Somehow, it throws their whole universe topsy-turvy. The resulting reaction to their world out of place is to make it right.

As an example, on a recent trip to Monterey, my brother-in-law, also a Virgo, straightened up a whole rack of tourist T-shirts because they weren't straight and the sizes were out of order. We left him in the store and went on with our shopping and told him to catch up with us when he was done. I would wager that the rack in that store was never better organized than after he left, and they didn't have to pay him a cent! His wife knew enough about his Virgo behavior to know she couldn't stop him, so she just browsed while he joyfully fixed what was wrong in his world. She reported to me the other day that he still does it all the time! The world would be so organized if we were all that way, but, unfortunately, we each have our own sign's weaknesses or strengths to deal with for us to always tolerate Virgos in our lives.

Another somewhat negative aspect of the Virgo is their ability to hold onto an idea that they think has merit, regardless of the other person's opinion. I say it is *somewhat* negative because it can also be an asset—it just depends if you are the beneficiary or the victim. Let me illuminate this for you a little. If there is a chore to be done, the Virgo may hound you until it is accomplished. This could be good or bad depending on how you handle being hounded. Doing the task immediately will certainly alleviate the pressure, but what if you don't have time do it immediately? Your Virgo will certainly remind you non-stop until you do.

Another example is when a Virgo gets some idea for you to better yourself. Remember that a Virgo wants the world to be perfect, so having you fit all the criteria for perfection is their goal. You may feel that things are fine and dandy, but you are delusional. No Virgo in their right mind would let an idea for making you better pass them by. You may find this somewhat irritating. You may actually think you're fine the way you are, but think again. The best method to avoid fighting over their suggestions is to just do it. Another method to avoid trouble is to walk away. This will work in the short term, but rest assured that your Virgo would bring it up over and over until you finally cave-in (or move into a cave!)

One of my grandsons, a Virgo, is always trying to come up with a solution for problems that he sees, even if you don't see it as a problem. If you don't like his first idea, he has several more waiting right behind it. Virgos like to make things right and they like to *be* right. They are the "fixers" of the universe!

Rule Number Three: <u>Virgos love confirmation of their perfection.</u> The easiest survival technique to use with your Virgo is to get out of the way and let them have at it. Why fight it, when you can get so much in return? I, for instance, have never been good at finances. I wisely let my wife take care of paying the bills and balancing the checkbooks. She does it so well that I would be a fool to try and change our arrangement. She gets as excited when she balances a checkbook without finding one error as I do about my favorite football team scoring a touchdown. We have three checking accounts to keep track of, one personal and one for each of our businesses. Sometimes, I think we have three accounts for her pleasure rather than any business reason. She not only takes care of our accounts, but also balances checkbooks for clients with as much pleasure as she does ours. As an Aquarius (well known to not care about such details), it can be difficult for me to understand her glee, but I know that she truly loves it, so I just get out of the way, let her have her fun, then I compliment her on her achievement, which makes it even better for her. **Rule Number Three: <u>Virgos love confirmation of their perfection.</u>**

The same perfectionist nature that keeps our checkbooks and finances in order helps my wife run a smooth and efficient business. The heart of her office services is her word processing. I have never seen anyone who can enter material with the speed and perfection that she does. I have known others who could type as fast or faster than her, but not with the same polish and lack of errors. She often tells potential clients who mention that another typing service is cheaper that they can either drive a Volkswagen or a Mercedes—it's their choice. The clients who have opted to go with the "Volkswagen" have usually come back to her for her "Mercedes" service after the "Volkswagen" service ended up costing them more because of mistakes or they weren't satisfied with the quality. Another of my wife's favorite sayings is, "You get what you pay for."

As I am writing, my wife prepares for a trip and gives me more material. Her perfectionist nature comes through in how she packs her suitcases. She has everything perfectly folded and wouldn't dream of mixing underwear and pants or letting her shoes (which are perfectly nested together) come into contact with anything else. I brought her a lint remover, knowing she couldn't leave home without one, and threw it into her suitcase, only to have her exclaim, "Don't put it in ***there*** like ***that***!" I replied, "Like it's going to hurt anything." She responded,

"Wellll!" I just smile knowingly, because I had disrupted her perfect universe once again.

I was wrapping a gift to be sent to one of my wife's friends, and I asked my wife which bow I should use. I showed her several examples, including one that was perfect for the box but wasn't in perfect condition. She said that for anyone else it would be fine, but her friend is also a Virgo and an imperfect bow would just not do. I used a new flawless bow on the present to pacify her. Never mind that I packed it in another box with flo-pack and shipped it nearly 3,000 miles, during which anything could happen. But when it left our house, it was perfect.

Virgos also use their perfectionist nature where sex is involved. I don't want to open any can of worms in my book, so suffice it to say that the person who benefits from this perfectionism can be very lucky. Of course, you need to learn all the survival techniques to get to the point where you can confirm what I am asserting. It can be well worth it. However, because of their perfectionist nature they may feel that they did it so well they don't need to do it so often. It's the age-old quandary of quality versus quantity. Enough said about that!

Chapter Two

WORKING WITH VIRGOS

Living with a Virgo is one thing because you have oftentimes made a conscious choice to do so, but working with a Virgo can be quite another matter. The first downside to working with a Virgo is that we often are unaware of (or simply don't care) what the signs of our co-workers are. We blunder into confrontations with Virgos unprepared for what may follow. Remember that Virgos like perfection (see Rule One), which can translate into a strained relationship at times. How to work with a Virgo can greatly depend on what position each of you holds.

The Virgo boss can be quite a handful to the uninitiated. My wife has a client at whose office she sometimes works because of his specialized computer system. This client is also a Virgo and the tales I hear are astounding. He is a perfectionist and expects his employees to also be perfectionists. As perfect as my wife tries to be, he has been known to go into tirades about things he perceives are not perfect. This has led to several employees moving on to greener, quieter pastures. Although he has improved recently by removing caffeine from his diet, he still has a tendency to get irate when things aren't perfect.

Working for someone like this can be very annoying, unless you learn how to deal with it. The best possible defense is to simply not make any mistakes. The next best defense is to merely admit that you were wrong and that you will try harder the next time. Whatever you do, do not try to defend yourself by justifying your mistakes, saying that you were too busy to get it right. My wife is fond of saying, "Why is it there's never enough time to do it right, but there's always enough time to do it over?" I am sure that this is a Virgo credo, because only a perfectionist could have come up with a statement like that. I do agree with the statement, it's just that only a perfectionist would come up with it.

I often find myself wondering what our world would be like if we all did things right the first time. A case in point is the automotive repair industry, which can be very good, very bad, or, most annoying of all, merely adequate. "Adequate," to me, is "just getting by." We took our Italian car to a dealer that is supposed to have the best factory-trained mechanics in our area. Their ***best*** consists of doing the work and causing other problems in the process. While putting in a door handle, they tore the leather on the door panel, glued it with Super Glue, and didn't even tell us. Another time, they fixed an electrical problem with our radio (which a month later broke again) and in the process somehow disconnected the car alarm. When confronted about these things, they insisted they didn't do it but would try to fix it. After leaving the car at their shop for a day, they accomplished nothing. We then had to pay someone else to fix it. Even though there were few mechanics in the area trained to work on this Italian car, we found a new place to go and never went back to the previous mechanic. The dealer lost thousands of dollars of our business because someone didn't take the time to do it right the first time. I would have to assume that if <u>our</u> work was being done poorly, then others must have had the same problem and moved on as well. Perhaps the dealer should hire a

Virgo to run the service center, not someone who "just gets by." I recently had occasion to stop by the dealer in question, and instead of having a full shop with cars waiting outside, there was only one car in the shop. Their lack of quality service appears to have hurt them significantly.

Rule Number Four: <u>Don't make mistakes!</u> Working for a Virgo is either a very frustrating or a very rewarding experience. The frustration comes from the demands that are made. The rewards come from the results that are generated. Working for a Virgo can cause you to stretch your own capabilities to do the job right, which leads to you becoming better at what you do. Knowing that my wife is going to proofread my work makes me a better writer, because I would prefer if there were no mistakes. But, like her client who valiantly tries to cheat the proofreader, I rarely get anything by her. She even found a mistake by the spellchecker in WordPerfect when it allowed a spelling of a word that she said was wrong. I tried to argue that if the spellchecker did not see the mistake, it must have two acceptable spellings. She insisted that I look it up in her six-inch-thick dictionary (a beloved gift from a former Virgo client), which contains every conceivable, acceptable variation on words. She was right and WordPerfect was wrong! Perhaps

WordPerfect needs a Virgo, like my wife, who can proofread their dictionary before it gets released.

Not only do Virgos dislike mistakes, but also they love to point them out to you. When a Virgo finds a mistake that you have created, they will revel in their discovery. This can either be very useful or very irritating. If you can handle being shown your mistakes without taking it personally, then you can learn from what a Virgo can reveal to you. If you take offense to being shown the errors of your ways, then you are in for a rough ride! Arguing with your Virgo boss will earn you nothing but grief. What the Virgo wants to hear is how grateful you are to them for showing you the error of your ways. They want to know that you see your mistakes, are willing to take responsibility for them, and make the necessary corrections to ensure that the same mistake doesn't occur again. They do not want to hear excuses or arguments to try and show them why you are right. What they want is to see no mistakes. Period! But in the real world there will be mistakes, so what our Virgo wants to hear is that you see the error of your ways and that you will correct it immediately. **Rule Number Four: <u>Don't make mistakes!</u>** (Or if you do, be prepared to admit them readily.)

Chapter Three

CLEANLINESS IS NEXT TO GODLINESS

*R*ule Number Five: <u>**Virgos like things nice and tidy.**</u> It may seem to be a tad redundant to say that Virgos like things neat and clean (you know, "A place for everything, and everything in its place). After all, wouldn't perfectionism lead to neatness? The answer is a resounding **YES!** But there are Virgos that do not fit this pattern. Some are actually slobs, but their need for order will surface somehow. Regardless of whether your Virgo is a neat freak or a slob, there is a real good reason to have a chapter devoted to cleanliness; it could save your marriage or your job. Virgos can tolerate other people's messiness, but not if they have to live with it. A very basic survival technique when dealing with a Virgo is to keep things neat and tidy.

I was recently honored when an Aquarian friend asked me to be best man at his wedding (to a Virgo). My friend was so busy running around making sure that things were right, I'm not sure he had time to be nervous. It was a beautiful wedding, held on Mt. Shasta in Northern California, at the highest point to which you could drive. His wife, also a very good friend, is a Virgo born on the same day and year as my wife. Her Virgoness was evident throughout the wedding and reception. She looked lovely in her white gown and was very careful not to get it dirty, not an easy feat given that the wedding took place on a flat, windy outcropping of dirt and rocks. We spent several hours up there, with a mini-reception held after the service, followed by a dinner reception in the town of Mt. Shasta later that day. The bride managed to stay extremely clean throughout the festivities. When it came time for the bride and groom to feed each other cake, they used forks! Now I'm not saying that there is anything wrong with this, but at every other wedding I have attended, the bride and groom eat the cake with their hands and generally smear each other's faces with cake. There was no smearing that day!

I turned to my wife and said, "Boy, is this a Virgo wedding or what?" I bet they talked about how to eat the cake beforehand and she probably let him know that if he smeared her with cake, he could talk to the divorce attorneys after the reception. Needless to say, it was a perfect wedding and reception. My friend is very smart. The last thing you want to do when marrying a Virgo is to start off on the wrong foot.

Another of my wife's favorite sayings is "I'm Clean Jean—I repel dirt." Once, as she was walking out of the door to leave on a trip, my wife managed to get a very small smudge of dirt on her otherwise white pants. This little speck of dirt almost caused her to miss her plane, because she ran back into the house to change clothes. Luckily, she couldn't find anything to wear because all of her other white pants were already packed, so she was back out in the car right away. She said she would just have to clean it off when she got to the airport, which she did immediately after I dropped her off. She is very fond of white, probably because it fits in so well with her Virgo sensitivity, but sometimes I wonder if that is such a good idea. White is so easy to get dirty that she is often upset when something gets on her clothing. Even her nickname, "Clean Jean," testifies to the way she envisions herself in her perfect world. "I'm Clean Jean—I never spill!" she exclaims following a near miss. The truth is, she rarely does spill or get dirty. It is just not in her nature to do so. **Rule Number Five: <u>Virgos like things nice and tidy</u>**.

Rule Number Six: <u>Don't fight it, just do it!</u> The Virgo penchant for cleanliness can be annoying to the uninitiated non-Virgos among us. Virgos see something dirty and can't get back on track, even if they are walking out the door. My wife was leaving to go to a client's the other day when she came out of the back of the house with her face all skewed up and told me that one of the cats had made a mess coming out of the litter box. I was in the middle of playing a video game (one of my weaknesses) and I calmly stated, "I'll take care of it in a minute." She gave me that wrinkled face look again and pro-claimed, "But it's *poop!*" I knew that it was hope-less for me to put it off, because she would not be able to leave knowing that there was *poop* loose in her house. It didn't matter that *I* knew I would take care of it, but it was imperative that *she* knew it was done. I gave her my best "Oh my God, you Virgos" look and proceeded to go take care of this horrible state of disorderliness—which, in her defense, was (for once) as bad as she made it out to be. I took care of the mess and she was able to go off happily to work. The term "cleanliness is next to Godliness" must have been created by a Virgo mother somewhere. I don't mean to insinuate that there is something wrong with wanting a mess cleaned up, but just that a Virgo's timetable is different than the rest of us. I would have cleaned up the ***poop*** after she left, when I was done with my game and when it was convenient for me. My wife was letting me know that there is a big distinction between seeing something that needs to be fixed and actually fixing it. ***She*** doesn't want to fix it; she just wants it fixed. It answered my long unanswered question of why it is when she sees something wrong that ***I*** am the one who gets the dubious honor of making it right. She is sort like Captain Pickard of <u>Star Trek: Next Generation</u> and I am Number Two, also of the aforementioned show (and not from the aforementioned cat). She says, "Make it so!" and I get to "Make it so!" In this case, Number Two really got to pick up number 2!

When you are married to a Virgo, Nike's advertising slogan "Just do it!" comes to mind. It is probably another Virgo saying. **Rule Number Six: <u>Don't fight it, just do it!</u>**

Rule Number Seven: <u>Survival is dependent on our being able to adapt to the Virgo environment</u>. My brother-in-law, Jim, is even more the typical Virgo than my wife. His house is spotless when we visit and we try to make sure not to alter his universe. He had just gotten new carpet before one of our visits and we had to take off our shoes every time we came into the house. Jim said that he would only be like this for the first year or so. I didn't have the heart to tell him that he had always been like that and would always be that way. On our last visit, two years later, we still had to take off our shoes. If it wasn't new carpet, then it would be that they were renting out a room and didn't want the new potential roommate to see it dirty, or company was coming, or one of a hundred other reasons why we had to be careful not to leave any signs of our existence. The pure and simple fact is that he is a Virgo. All of the other reasons would be totally insignificant without that. Virgoness drives a Virgo to do what he does, not the circumstance.

Jim's youngest daughter married a Virgo (after having been raised by a Virgo), so she was trained to live with his quirkiness. Jim and his son-in-law are so very similar that **they** don't even notice. Our twin great-nieces, however, were sorely unprepared for their first visit to their aunt's house after she married a Virgo. When they went to visit, they relayed to us the tales of being a guest in a Virgo's house. They had to take off their shoes (more new carpet) and had to be extremely careful not to make any messes. A spill could destroy an otherwise happy visit. They were so distraught after their first visit, they weren't sure they ever wanted to visit again. They have since gotten over it, of course, but won't forget it.

Visiting a Virgo is only temporary, but Virgos have to live with themselves forever! Virgos can even drive **themselves** crazy with their Virgo ways. My wife has been known to say "Sometimes I wish I weren't such a Virgo so I could get things done quicker" when her strict attention to detail causes her twice as long to finish something.

Other Virgo mates have told me that they tell their spouse they are right, even if they don't believe it, just to keep the peace. It saves a lot of time and antacid. Having an understanding of Virgos may save you a lot of frustration, but it doesn't eliminate it all. When a Virgo wants things a certain way, your best hope for survival is simply to accept it, no matter how absurd **you** think it is. Only **they** know why they want it that way, and they usually have a good reason for it. My wife calls it a Virgo's reason! There are simply too many Virgos around to avoid them. **Rule Number Seven: <u>Survival is dependent upon our being able to adapt to the Virgo environment.</u>**

Chapter Four

THE VIRGO CHILD

I was not intending to include any mention of the Virgo child until I was talking to a friend about my book and how many Virgos there are. She said that one of her daughters is a Virgo, and we began to talk about her daughter's tendencies to be organized. She said that when she was two years old, she wouldn't leave the house until all of her toys were put away in their proper place. She would even take the time to very carefully put every Lego back in their can, which she was discouraged from doing because it would cause all of them to be late. Eventually, she stopped doing it, but her mother has noticed that there seems to be something missing in her daughter's life. The

mother began to recognize that her daughter's Virgoness might be something to encourage. In fact,
she began to see that she had not been providing
the proper environment for her to excel. Remember that a Virgo thrives in an environment that is
well organized and stagnates in an environment
that is disorganized. I believe that she plans to
encourage her daughter's Virgoness now that she
is aware of the effects of not doing so.

Virgos will display their unhappiness with
their surroundings in many ways. My friend's
daughter gets very sullen because she feels that
the world doesn't understand her and she doesn't
know why. The Virgo believes the world should
work perfectly, and they don't understand why everyone else doesn't. This can lead to a great deal
of unhappiness if not addressed. The Virgo child
doesn't know why he/she does what they do. They
just do it!

On the day that my friend and I talked, her
daughter was in the living room organizing and
running activities for the other children. Baby-
sitting is the perfect activity for the Virgo child.
The Virgo child loves to be in charge. If you have
more than one Virgo child, you need to learn to
delegate activities so that each child is in charge
of something. This will lead to a much happier

environment than giving all the responsibility to the oldest child. Each Virgo must feel that he or she is in control to some degree, which will lead to a harmonious household.

Another couple that is a Virgo/Aquarian pairing related to me how being dirty affects their relationship. The wife, who is the Virgo, cannot stand to be dirty. If she gets one little spot on her clothes, it is such a distraction for her that she has to change immediately! She told me that she is sure "everyone" will see the spot. She relates that as a child of five years old, she was already developing strong Virgo traits. On a vacation trip to the beach, she refused to wear a swimsuit that had been used on a previous day, so when she ran out of clean suits she just stopped going to the beach. Today, how she presents herself is very important.

Rule Number Eight: <u>Virgos love organization.</u> It is imperative in the growth of the Virgo child that the parents understand what makes their child tick. When you understand what makes your child do what they do, it can make it easier to interact with them in a manner that will encourage them to do things that will make them happy, even if it is something that you wouldn't do yourself. A parent who has a Virgo child will find that their child actually may enjoy straightening up their room or organizing the silverware drawer. Then again, the Virgo child may want it organized but wants someone else to do it. Activities that may seem like a chore to non-Virgos can actually be fun to a Virgo. For example, if you have a Virgo child who excels at math, perhaps you should have **them** balance your checkbook. The Virgo child may actually find this to be a fun activity, and you might be surprised at how well they could do it. Other activities that the Virgo child might find interesting that we would never think of might include: folding and putting away clothes, organizing closets or drawers, rearranging kitchen cupboards, cleaning the garage, or any other activity that involves organizing. Tasks like these don't necessarily sound like fun to most of us, but to a Virgo, if approached properly, they can be very entertaining. Never use these activities as a punishment, because this could cause a tremendous amount of turmoil for the Virgo child. **Rule Number Eight: Virgos love organization.**

The Virgo finds that serving people is very entertaining and self-satisfying. They enjoy being in charge of projects and would love nothing more than to show what they can do. Give a Virgo child the opportunity to baby-sit other children and you will be surprised at how much fun they will have organizing things for them to do. In groups such as Boy Scouts, Girl Scouts, school politics, and other young persons' groups, the Virgo child will thrive if given responsibility and stagnate if left out of the loop. Perhaps this seems like it would be unfair to the other children they interact with, but not many other children would complain if the Virgos <u>want</u> to do all the work. Virgos are perfect candidates to run a bake sale, candy sale, or to organize a car wash. Any activity that will allow the Virgo child to bring out their organizational skills or serve others will make them very happy.

I had mentioned earlier in my book how Virgos surround me. That Virgo community recently grew by two. My wife had to give up her baby son at birth many years ago, due to familial pressure and the social stigma that an unwed mother had to face in 1967. She did so reluctantly and only agreed to it after being convinced that it was better for the child. She **never** forgot about him, literally thinking of him every day at 1:56 p.m. (the time of his birth) and, of course, on his birthday, Christmas, Mother's Day, etc. She had been trying to find him almost since the day she gave him up. She tried private investigators, writing to Ann Landers, and finally the Internet. Four or five years after putting it on the Internet, her son found her! We are now proud parents of not one, but two wonderful young men, Johnny and David. Johnny's adoptive family gave birth to David six years after Johnny's adoption, and since their parents are no longer in the picture, we became parents to both of them. In the bargain, we also acquired three of the nicest, most beautiful daughters-in-law that you could ask for, Bette, Tammy and Lauren. That's not all. Johnny and his wife, Tammy, along with his ex-wife Bette, are raising our four wonderful grandchildren: Carole Ann, Donald, Josh, and Chrissy. I bring all of this up for more than just being proud to be a father and grandfather. Two of our new grandchildren are Virgos! What do you suppose are the odds of that happening? I now have two boys to help inspire me with my writing about Virgo children. At this writing, Josh is eleven years old and Donald is thirteen. I hope to have many years to study these two fine boys to see how well my theories about Virgos work.

When I told Tammy about some of the traits that Virgos have about being neat, she said that didn't fit with Josh and Donald. I believe that as she reads this, she will find more things that fit for them than she thinks. Children who are Virgos are just growing into their Virgoness. It is something that will develop as time goes by. The techniques that we have discussed may make it easier to raise them. Since we plan to spend as much time as possible with our grandchildren, I hope to have a little influence on how they adapt to being Virgos and how the family adapts to them. Remember that just because a Virgo likes order and cleanliness, it doesn't always mean that *they* want to do the work. After all, kids are kids, and playing the latest video game is more interesting than cleaning their room. But try moving a few treasures around in their room and see what reaction you get. Johnny's technique is to throw away the things they leave lying around. Eventually they will learn that being organized has its own rewards and they will begin to see how it fits with their Virgoness. Of course, they may still seek out someone who will do the straightening up for them, but that doesn't mean that they won't learn my wife's favorite saying, "A place for everything and everything in its place." It is important to note that not every Virgo child will respond equally to these techniques. My two grandsons do not fit all of the typical traits of a Virgo. That is to say, they don't fit all of the positive traits. It is important to remember that Virgos may have a dark side to their nature, just like the rest of us.

When queried about the Virgo nature of her sons, my daughter-in-law said that they didn't fit the mold. I asked her why she felt this was so, and she responded that they were very messy in their bedroom. I thought about this for a while and realized that this does not negate their desire for order. They want things in order; they just don't want to do the work. They actually display quite a few Virgo traits. They take frequent showers. They both dress themselves well and spend a great deal of time making sure their hair is just right. I find that for an eleven and thirteen year old, that constitutes a great deal of neatness. They also display a trait that I had only seen from my wife before: they eat one item of food on their plate until it is gone and then eat the next item. Their response to my inquiry about this behavior was that they don't like to mix the foods because it ruins the individual tastes. I don't know many people who eat that way, except Virgos. Perhaps I am wrong, but don't most people you know take a bite of one item and then a bite of another and sometimes even mix two things together in the same bite?

Finding our family and finding out that two Virgo grandchildren exist also bolstered my theory about there being more Virgos out there than the other signs. Granted, Johnny had Josh from a previous marriage and Tammy had Donald from a previous marriage, but it still brings home the fact that Virgos are everywhere!

Chapter Five

TRAVELING WITH A VIRGO

Going on a vacation with your favorite Virgo can be a rewarding and frustrating experience at the same time. I usually let my wife make our travel arrangements for two very good reasons. First, she is a stickler for details and will always make sure to cover all contingencies that might occur. Secondly, she would get really mad if I made the plans and forgot something. It is much safer to let her make the arrangements and take the responsibility for any errors she might make than it is for me to make the arrangements and take the heat for my errors. Of course, it also gives *me* wonderful ammunition in the rare event *she* makes an error or overlooks something!

Any change or error in a trip sends a Virgo into a tizzy. I have been traveling for years, including extensive trips to Europe and the Middle East. I have had layovers of up to eight hours and even had a flight booked that no longer existed, which led to having to spend the night in Beirut, Lebanon, at the airline's expense when I was seventeen years old and traveling alone. These experiences have prepared me for any number of delays or inconveniences when traveling. My wife, on the other hand, has very little experience with travel, so small errors become big problems when she is traveling with me. The old nickname "Nervous Nelly" could easily apply to my wife. On a recent trip to Catalina Island, we had to make several changes to our itinerary in the middle of our trip. We changed the flight for our return trip three times before we departed Los Angeles for San Francisco, and each time there was the accompanying rushing around to get to the right gate. My wife would ask the ticket agent a question, and before the answer was even given she would ask another. It seemed to me that we spent an inordinate amount of time getting information. Then when we got to the gate she wanted to change again. We ended up getting to San Francisco twenty minutes early, but we had to wait twenty minutes for our luggage to arrive. The flight we ended up on was packed to the gills. The jet was an old one with lousy ventilation and cramped seats. We found out from another traveler who came in on the plane with our luggage that his flight (our original flight) was nearly empty and they were treated like kings. We could have saved ourselves a lot of time and trouble by just staying with our original flight.

I know that I am not always the most reasonable man on earth, but travel with a Virgo can make me even worse. I just want to get from point A to point B with the least amount of hassle. If a stairway is closed that leads to the luggage carousel, I will just follow the signs to the next stairway, but my wife will ask the passing flight crew how to get there. She calls me "Moses" and says that like most men I never ask for directions, and I say she asks for too many. I suppose that the best technique for dealing with this Virgo desire to have a map for everything is to just let them have their way. It surely beats the heck out of being wrong and having to admit it to your Virgo. It just gives them too many points to play with.

One acquaintance of ours told us how worried she gets when she travels. She worries so much about things going wrong that on a trip to Seattle she booked a room through a travel agent and then booked another room online. By worrying so much, she ended up paying for two rooms. Ouch!

There are good aspects to the Virgo traveler as well. My wife always figures out what our expenses will be and budgets our trips well. We always have money available for emergencies because she will stow away some cash in a secret place so that if anything happens we will be ready for it. My wife will also bring everything but the kitchen sink. This is a plus because we usually have what we need, but it is a minus because the luggage can be quite excessive and heavy. My chiropractor is getting rich from fixing me after a trip!

Our trip to Catalina was with our friends who are also a Virgo and Aquarius pairing. Upon arriving at the condo where we were staying, we all went off to our respective rooms to unpack. I had unpacked my bags, put everything away, and was relaxing and reading while Jean and Susan (the two Virgos) put their things in order. What had taken me five minutes took them at least a half an hour. In both their rooms and bathrooms, everything was laid out in perfect order, with taller products lined up behind smaller products. I did not look through all their drawers and closets, but I know that they were in perfect order as well. While it is true that my items were just placed in the drawers and not particularly organized, I much prefer relaxing on my vacations, rather than spending my time getting organized. I never had one bit of trouble finding my underwear and socks or toothbrush, even though I had spent a fraction of the time they had. They even commented <u>in unison</u> that I had unpacked way too fast for their tastes. Virgos are funny that way. They even get irritated if someone else doesn't unpack "right."

Going out to eat with a Virgo is another thing all together. I pride myself on selecting what I want from a menu in record time compared to most people. Not only do I pick fast, but often what I choose ends up being more desirable than what others chose. It wasn't always that way for me. As I mentioned earlier, I have had extensive training in what I referred to as Zen-like training. I studied for five years with Grand Master Ji Han Jae, the top-ranked martial artist in Hapkido, a Korean martial art, during which time I received my second-degree black belt. I meditated for an hour a day, worked out for two hours a day, and completely altered the foods I ate. I was a Warrant Officer in the Civil Air Patrol for two years. I always took pride in how my uniform looked. Military training is a good place to prepare for being married to a Virgo. I took the *est* training in 1979 and worked with the organization for over five years. I learned to manage large numbers of people and became very organized and tidy. Werner Erhardt, the founder of *est*, was a stickler for creating a "safe space" in which to perform his trainings. We were trained to be very Zen-like in our approach to things. As a logistics supervisor, I could spot a speck of lint on the floor of a training room from twenty feet away that others had just walked over. It would literally glow.

One of the premises of *est* was the notion of choice. Choice is defined as selecting freely after consideration. Choosing for many is a chore. For me it has become relatively easy. If the choice is chocolate or vanilla, I just choose one. If there are more than two selections, then I generally go through the available choices and choose one. I have had great success with this method in choosing everything from the food I eat to the clothes I wear. I look at the choices and choose. I looked at the menu, asked if the sand dabs were good, got an affirmative response, and ordered them forthwith.

Going out to dinner with a Virgo is like going out with an alien when this is how you operate. Go out with **two** Virgos and Mars might well have invaded the earth! A Virgo not only has to spend an inordinate amount of time choosing, but also then wants to make alterations to how their choice is prepared. If my wife sees something that strikes her fancy but it contains something she doesn't want, she will ask the waitress to ask the chef to make it **her** way. The answer 99 percent of the time is "no." That then leads to her perusing the menu again for another choice. The next choice also has an unwanted item and the process is repeated. Having been in the business of selling to chefs for years and spending a great deal of time behind the scenes in kitchens gives me a better understanding of how a food service establishment works. The one thing I know for certain is that a chef hates substitutions. He/she generally created the dish in question, and asking for him/her to change it is akin to a slap in the face. Even if he/she wanted to accommodate our Virgo diner, it is often impossible to do so without considerable extra work. Chefs come to work well before the restaurant opens to prepare their recipes. They have people who aid them in cutting and prepping the ingredients, preparing sauces, and cooking the food. Imagine that you have been working hard all day to get a gourmet meal prepared and someone says they love pepper steak but could you leave off the pepper, or that they love clam chowder but can't eat potatoes. Chefs are not known for being calm and understanding. (No offenses to chefs because I know, like, and understand them well.) The waitress who takes such a request to a chef is not likely to be greeted well. A Virgo diner will not take any of these factors into consideration when they ask the waitress to change a dish to satisfy them. Remember that to a Virgo the world should be perfect, including getting things their way when they go out to eat. My Virgo companions that night in Catalina made such requests, only to be informed that they couldn't make changes. For a Virgo to choose from a menu where no alterations are available is like pulling their own teeth without Novocaine.

It is never unusual to pass by my wife while she makes up her mind what to order, but when there are two Virgos involved it was like watching a tennis match. Susan and Jean passed the waitress back and forth like a good volley. Luckily our waitress turned out to be a Virgo herself and took our orders like water off a log. What are the odds that you would go to an island only to end up with a restaurant full of Virgo diners and get served by a Virgo waitress? Needless to say, when our order arrived everything was absolutely perfect! This scenario is an exception. You won't find many restaurants that respond well to substitutions. One friend related how she orders: plain hamburger and fries with nothing else, meat only without sauces, peanut butter sandwiches without jelly, and no Chinese food. Things just can't get much more specific. When your Virgo displays such behavior, don't get mad.

On a very recent trip, just after I sent this book to press, an incident occurred that exemplifies Virgos so well I had to have it added. My wife and I were on a trip to Portland, Oregon for one of my conventions. Ten of us had decided to go on a dinner river cruise. Before you board the boat, they take a picture of each couple with a life preserver which has the name of the boat, "The Portland Spirit," on it. We all had a wonderful dinner and evening. Towards the end of the cruise, they bring the pictures to you to decide if you wish to buy them. It was a wonderful memory to keep, so we all purchased them. My wife, our "Virgo on the job," noticed that they had misspelled Spirit on our picture. Of all of the couples at our table, only *she* noticed and only *she* decided to send it back. When the girl brought back our corrected picture, my wife now noticed that the date said Friday, September, 16th 2005. There was no way she could accept an error like that! She called the girl over again and showed her the error. For a second time our picture was sent back to be corrected. When the young lady returned our picture, everything was corrected; however, now the name of the boat on the life preserver was faded. She was going to send it back again, but I convinced her that we might not make it back to shore if we did. The girl with the pictures said that not one other person had noticed the error in "Spirit" all day long, and no one else sent their picture back for correction. Nitpicking is just the Virgo way. She couldn't have **not** sent it back, any more than she could have gone on the boat with a spot on her clothes. It just isn't possible. I had to almost restrain her to keep her from sending it back again. The Virgo does what they do as compulsion. Everybody had a good laugh about Jean's behavior, but no one else had to have things corrected. Virgos insist on things being right. Maybe everyone else should have. After all, when you pay for something, it should be right; but if they had, we might have been there all night!

Rule Number Nine: <u>Don't get mad, get used to it!</u> I don't want my comments regarding Virgos to come out as too negative, because as I have stated before there are a lot of good aspects to living with a Virgo, it's just that sometimes it can get to you. My wife has a tendency to walk out of the room when I don't agree with her. She feels that if I *don't* agree, then we are having a fight. That makes me angry, and then we really do have a fight. Of course, it's hard to have a fight when the person you are having a fight with leaves the room. I get over a fight usually before she does because it's in my nature to do so, but other people might not act the same as I do. There really is no place for anger when dealing with your favorite Virgo. Your anger will never make up for a lack of understanding. **Rule Number Nine: <u>Don't get mad, get used to it!</u>**

We really had a good time that night at the restaurant in Catalina surrounded by Virgos. Once you are aware of what makes a Virgo tick, it becomes much easier to deal with them on a day-to-day basis. This book is specifically written to share what I have learned about Virgos so that your experience of them will be a rewarding one. Your trips will be better, your home will be better, your workplace will be better, and your sex will be better if you learn to not get mad at your favorite Virgo. And then after dinner, we played games!

Chapter Six

PLAYING GAMES

B eing the partner with a Virgo while playing a game can be rewarding and frustrating at the same time. It should come as no surprise that Virgos like to win. Winning just fits with their perfectionist nature. My wife and I love to play games, but we seem to do better when we play against each other than we do as partners. We have had exceptionally good fun with a game called <u>Sequence,</u> a card game in which you place colored chips on a board corresponding to the card you play. The object is to get two sequences of five cards on the board when you are playing two or four players. (The rules vary slightly for other combinations of players.) There is two of every card on the board and in the deck. The exception to that are the Jacks, which are in the deck, but not on the board. The one-eyed Jack removes one of your opponent's chips from the board and a two-eyed Jack is wild. When playing with a partner, the object is to try and play the cards that will coincide with what your partner has in their hand. This can be rather tricky at times because you may play a card in a spot where you think it will do good, but your partner had other plans. Sometimes, you may have four cards in a row in your hand but be missing the fourth. Then your partner plays the card you were missing, but on the wrong place on the board. The point is that unless you are clairvoyant or cheating, it is unlikely you will know what card your partner has or is going to play. My wife hates to lose! After losing the first game to our friends, she began to get a tad testy. After losing our second game, she started to give me dirty looks. By the time we lost our third and fourth game to our friends, one of whom had never played and the other whom had played rarely, she became downright belligerent! She would give me such a look when I played my card in the wrong place (in her viewpoint). Her comments got more and more pointed until we began to argue over how we were playing. Our friends, a Virgo and an Aquarian, were chortling with glee at their victories and the fact that our team was falling apart, which did nothing but add to my wife's frustration. According to her, I was talking too much, I wasn't paying attention, and I was playing in the wrong places. It didn't matter that my next card would win the game and I had no card to stop them with as they finished us off with another victory. It was a matter of her not liking to lose. After the fourth game, we had to call it quits because Catalina Island was getting too small for the two of us.

I used to think that *I* was competitive and hated to lose, that is until I married my wife. We played chess once (and I do mean only ***once***) and she managed to win, even though I had superior forces and she was on the run. In the most crucial part of the game, the doorbell rang and I had to go answer it. When I came back, I had completely lost my concentration and blundered right into her trap. She won the game and has since refused to play me. She even goes so far as to tell people that I have never beaten her at chess. This infuriates me, because I know I am a good player and I believe I would have won had I not been interrupted. My Virgo doesn't like to lose and she won't play me again, because she knows that I would probably beat her. She says it is because now I know her strategy and it only works once. I say, "Then you don't really know how to play chess, because chess is about adapting." Of course, when she reads this, her Virgo pride may force her out of retirement so I can smash her into oblivion. I'm sure she will say it will never happen, but that's because she won't play again. Aquarians don't like to lose either!

Lots of people enjoy putting together jigsaw puzzles, but to the Virgo it is just a continuation of life itself! Virgos love order and anything that emphasizes that love is sure to be a winning combination. Putting together a puzzle is a fun activity that requires the ability to organize and recognize what goes where. My wife has putting puzzles together down to a science. It centers her and makes her relaxed and happy. First, she locates the edge pieces and constructs the frame, and then she fills in the middle by finishing one area before shifting to another, along the way placing pieces in other areas if she happens to see them or remember them from prior perusing. I realize that others may operate the same way, because it makes sense to do so, but not with the same organizational glee that she gets. She is fast and methodical and doesn't like too many hands helping her. If you happen along and give her some help, she will thank you to an extent, but woe to the person who takes over her puzzle. While we were on our vacation in Catalina, she brought a puzzle and started on it on the dining room table. Our friends would come over and give her a hand, which was fine, but then they would continue to work on it even after she said on several occasions that they were doing too much and leaving nothing for her. They would laugh and think she was just kidding, but I knew better. Putting together a puzzle is *her* fun activity and she doesn't want anyone else to finish it. Our friends were wise enough to leave her enough to finish so that she was satisfied. Even so, she was not happy that they had helped her so much. There is a very fine line between having fun with a Virgo and getting in their way.

Lily Armyann 2005

Chapter Seven

VIRGOS IN THE MILITARY

*V*irgos are organized, disciplined people, as we have seen previously, which makes them a perfect match for the military. A Virgo would find the clean, well-organized military base a safe refuge from the rest of the disorganized world around them. In the military, everyone is striving to keep things the way a Virgo likes it. A very strong Virgo personality would take to the military like a fish to water. What better place could there be than a place where everything is in its place and there is a place for everything? The only thing a Virgo should find abhorrent is the ideology, if it goes against their personal belief system. If the purpose of the military does not bother the Virgo, then a career in the military could be just the place for them.

My military experience is comprised of two years in the Civil Air Patrol, a subsidiary of the United States Air Force. I was fourteen when I joined a squadron in Beaumont, Texas. Whereas the CAP is not the Air Force, we had to wear Air Force uniforms and do many of the same things that are done in the military, including a yearly trip to a one-week boot camp at an Air Force base. We went on numerous search and rescue mission practices and a few real search and rescue missions during my stay in the CAP. Drilling, saluting, and looking proper were all included in our weekly meetings, which included the serious study of flying on the way to getting our pilots licenses. I still look back fondly on those days in uniform.

I was recalling my limited experience with the military to my wife the other day when it struck me that a Virgo would find that type of lifestyle to be right up their alley. I described to her how we managed to keep our socks pulled up and our shirt tails tucked in by connecting elastic garters that we made to our socks in the front and back, and running them up to our shirt tails. The result of these garters was to keep our uniforms always looking sharp. My mother (after all, I was only fourteen) would iron my uniforms with enough starch that they could almost stand up by themselves, with nice creases in the pants and shirts. I would spit polish my shoes until they could almost pass for patent leather. At fourteen I was already 6'4" in my stocking feet and I looked very military indeed. With my ribbons displayed proudly and my Warrant Officer emblems on my collars, it would have been hard for anyone to detect that I wasn't in the military. I was actually mistaken for an officer at an Air Force base once when I had my flight jumpsuit on, a present from a neighbor who had been a pilot in the Air Force, which I found out later was only worn by pilots who were all officers. I couldn't figure out why all of these guys kept saluting me as I walked across the base, until they came and told me that I shouldn't impersonate an officer. I bring all of this up to show that I do have a little knowledge of the workings of the military, although, I admit, not as much as someone who has actually been in the military. If I overstep any boundaries of etiquette or say anything that isn't completely accurate about the military, please keep that in mind. My wife loved every minute of my description of how I looked. I knew that it fit with her Virgo mentality.

In the military, a Virgo would have a chance to really show off their stuff. What Virgo wouldn't drool at the opportunity to live in a place where people are actually *made* to conform to something that Virgos find second nature. Having everything neat and tidy is a way of being to a Virgo. I imagine a Virgo walking across a military base and thinking that this must be what heaven is like. Even the rocks are clean and painted white. Perfect! When they arrive at the barracks with its shiny floors, clean latrines, and beds made so well you can bounce a quarter off of them . . . well, you can just imagine seeing that glazed look enter their eyes. This experience would be akin to a child in a candy store.

The Virgo desire for everything in order would be satiated often while in the military. Everything from paperwork to marching would add to the Virgo experience of utopia. If the military were smart, they would seek out those Virgos among them and nurture those qualities that make Virgos what they are.

Virgos are not known to be great military leaders (perhaps war makes the world imperfect), so if being an officer is part of their dream, then they may be disappointed. Out of a long list of famous Virgos, there was not one military genius. Virgos are much better at following than leading. If they can just enjoy the perfection of military life, then they may find that it fits them well.

Though Virgos may not necessarily be good military leaders, I believe that given the right position they would excel. They would especially be effective as officers or non-commissioned officers in such fields of endeavor as running the motor pool, the PX (base store), supply requisition, or accounting. Any position where their organizational skills can thrive and be encouraged (and nothing gets messed-up) would be a place they would enjoy.

Obviously the female military type would be well suited as a secretary or nurse. Their penchant for neatness and orderliness would be well suited for those positions, not that they wouldn't also do well in the previously mentioned areas. The military is, after all, an equal opportunity employer (and I don't mean to stir-up any feminists).

Chapter Eight

VIRGOS IN THE MEDIA

There seems to be no end to the jokes and characters on television and in movies that are directly related to the Virgo way of being. Those of us who are not Virgos find much to laugh about at the expense of Virgos. The character of Monica on <u>Friends</u> is probably the most complete Virgo of them all. In one episode, she actually washed dirty cars on her block because someone was coming to her home and she didn't like all the dirty cars in the way. There have been whole episodes devoted to her strange behavior. Years ago, in the early years of <u>Friends</u>, before Chandler and Monica got together, there was an episode in-

volving her known fixation for everything being in
its place. Monica's roommate, Rachel, decided to
try and please Monica by cleaning the apartment.
With all of her other friends present, Monica
shows that she is the epitome of a Virgo by noticing that an ottoman had been moved. She gets
a frantic look on her face, pretending that she is
considering leaving it where it is, when she clearly
intends to move it back. She says, "Yes, it could
go there, but let's just see how it looks back where
it was. There, that's better!" she exclaims. Her
friends then confront her about her behavior and
tell her that she can't just leave things where they
are and be wacky. She says she can. The show
ends with someone noticing that she has left her
shoes in the middle of the living room floor. She
says she will just leave them there because she is a
kook. As the credits roll, Monica lies in bed with
her eyes wide open contemplating her wayward
shoes. She considers getting up to get them so she
can go to sleep, but realizes that her friends will
confront her on her behavior. Her internal battle
rages to the point where she thinks to herself that
she could go and pick them up and then get up
real early to put them back before anyone notices.
She rolls over and yells to herself that she needs
help. Monica cannot change her spots any more
than a leopard can. She is a Virgo. She can't help

herself. Even if the writers did not intend for her to be a Virgo, she is one. And apparently so is her mother, because during all this she says, "I'm turning into MOM!"

Years have passed and now Chandler is Monica's new roommate, but apparently he has forgotten about the previous incident because he decides to move <u>everything</u> and clean the apartment. Ross comes in to the apartment in the middle of the cleaning and laughs that Monica is going to kill Chandler. Upon realizing that Ross is right, Chandler goes crazy trying to put things back into place. He fails, because he could never put things back <u>exactly</u> where they were. Luckily for Chandler, Monica has grown a great deal since her earlier days and she handled it quite well for a Virgo, but she still knew everything had been moved! Chandler should never make that mistake again, because he has now learned firsthand what it is like to live with a Virgo. That's not to say that there are not a multitude of opportunities left for the writers regarding Monica's behavior, just that they can't rewrite the same scenario again. Given the Virgo characteristics that we have looked at in this book, it should be easy to find fodder for jokes.

It would be easy to confuse Niles Crane's character on <u>Frasier</u> with Monica's Virgoness, but I believe that the writers were leaning more towards anal-retention when they created him. His impeccable style of dress, his fussiness about dusting off a chair before he sits down, and his other mannerisms lead us to believe that he has a profound psychological problem. Obviously, when they were creating the show about psychiatrists, an anal-retentive psychiatrist fit into their plans for a humorous character. There is plenty of the same kind of jokes used about Niles as there have been for years about anal-retentive. Even if people do not understand what makes an anal-retentive tick, they still find plenty to laugh about when an anal-retentive does his thing. Where I think the line becomes blurred is when the characteristics of the Virgo are compared with the anal-retentive. There can be many of the same characteristics involved: the constant fussiness, having things in their place, cleanliness, and being obsessed with something. Who knows, maybe Freud's entire test subjects were Virgos. That would blow all his data to pieces.

Even some of the people who are involved in the media in one way or another are or have been Virgos. Mostly people in the media comprise the list of famous Virgos. They include such notables as Michael Jackson (hmm, what a surprise), Raquel Welch, Sophia Loren, Sean Connery, Regis Philbin (we all knew that, right?), Tuesday Weld, Elliot Gould, Charlie Sheen, Richard Gere, Gloria Estefan, Bob Newhart, Peter Sellers, Michael Keaton, David Arquette, Adam Sandler, and Hugh Grant. As you can see from the list, these are people who are not only well dressed and tidy, but perfectionists at their art. This is by no means a complete list. I would fill a whole chapter if I were to list them all. Think of what the world would have been like without these Virgos using their Virgoness to create the entertaining things they have done for us. I think we can look forward to more Virgos in the media in the future.

Chapter Nine

VIRGOS AND THE HOLIDAYS

Virgos are caring, loving people for whom the holidays may represent a multitude of things. One thing in particular that a Virgo can shine at is organizing your holidays. Regardless of your religious affiliation or which holidays we are referring to, the Virgo can add their special flair to the holidays. In our house we celebrate Christmas with a lot of accessories. It is necessary to pack and unpack all of our "stuff" with care, lest anything should get broken. My wife is a stickler about how things should be done. I learned quickly that my old method of putting away Christmas was not going to pass muster with my wife, so I get out of the way and let her pack and unpack. This saves me a lot of frustration. She does her thing and I do the decorating. It's a match made in heaven. Whereas Virgos love to organize, Aquarians love to be creative. I love to decorate and she loves to organize. What could be better?

I do a tremendous amount of decorating at Christmas, which means that there is a lot to organize. Somehow, it never seems to be a mess. Each step is just that, a step. We don't haphazardly throw things around and eventually end up with a masterpiece. Rather, we start out with a masterpiece of organization and transfer it to the masterpiece that is our decorated house.

The real holiday organization ribbon, however, goes to my wife, "Clean Jean the Cookie Queen," in her cookie factory. She is in her Virgo glory during one of the most hectic times of the year. She has dozens of cans, lined up and sorted by person or family. She has a system devised so that she can pump out eighty dozen perfect chocolate chip cookies. Not only are her cookies the best in taste, but also she makes them all the same size. Of course, any "rejects" or "amoeba-like" ones go into my pile—just one of those things I *must* endure (oh the misery of it all!). I also get *too* many of the "good" ones, but they are *all* good to me. I gain about five pounds every year! She then proceeds to sort them into the cans in a dazzling display and deliver them to the lucky recipients. Yummm!

My wife also keeps track of all the names of friends, business associates, neighbors, and family that we need to buy gifts for. She almost never misses a birthday. I don't mean just birthdays of family members, but birthdays of almost every acquaintance that we have. They don't all get gifts, but the cards we purchase could probably keep a small card store in business! She has tried to pass on her skills at this to others, but it never works. She bought several special occasion calendars for friends and family, but they forget to use them. ("You can lead a horse to water, but you can't make it drink.") People may want to keep track of such things; it's just that for most of us it's not in our nature. It is in the Virgo's nature. Virgos' penchant for organization just enhances their caring nature. If my wife had the money to buy every acquaintance a gift for Christmas, then I think she would do so because it would save her a tremendous amount of time making cookies, but then there would be all of those disappointed faces on Christmas morning, as they opened their gifts and found them lacking the most anticipated gift of the season: "Clean Jean The Cookie Queen" chocolate chip cookies! One year she tried to skip giving cookies to everyone. Even though she bought them nice gifts, she was still assailed by choruses of "But where are *my cookies*?"

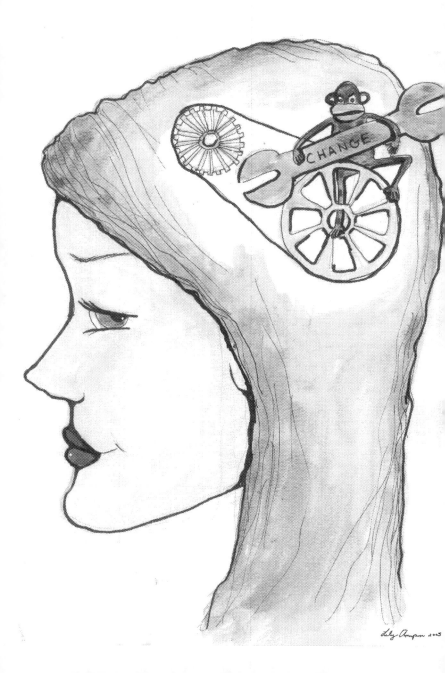

Chapter 10

VIRGOS AND CHANGE

*R*ule Number Ten: <u>**Change causes upset.**</u> Not just for Virgos, but for everyone (especially if you didn't get any cookies). The Virgos penchant for "a place for everything and everything in its place" makes them even more upset about change than the rest of us. All of us react to things around us that we have grown accustomed to, only to have it changed. Whereas, most of us go through a little discomfort from change, a Virgo's very being is upset by change.

My wife owned a 1975 Datsun 280Z for 22 years which she bought brand new right off the showroom floor, and she was very attached to it.

She remembers the day she bought that car as being the happiest day of her life. The car had a stereo 8-track player and she had quite an extensive collection of 8-track tapes. When her car was broken into in the 80's and the 8-track player was stolen, would she replace it with a newer, more modern cassette player? No, not my wife. She insisted on having a new 8-track player installed. After all, what would she do with all of her 8-track tapes if she had a cassette player? This was not a change she was willing to make.

After 22 years of owning her beloved 280Z, being decorated and driven in numerous Fog Fest parades, the heater and air conditioning not working for years, still having an 8-track player (years after they quit making 8-track tapes), a few (she made me say *a few*) minor rust spots, and other worn-out or out-dated items on it, circumstances forced us to sell her beloved car. It was very traumatic for her. She cried before, during, and after the sale of her car. The loss is still a bitter pill for her to swallow. Never mind that she got to have my luxury car, a 1992 Alfa Romeo 164L, because no amount of modern gadgets and comfort could ease the pain of her loss. Several years have passed since she sold the Z, but it still bothers her. I believe that the great majority of us would get over it far more quickly. I have fond memories of many of my old cars, even my first car that used to fill with smoke as we drove down the road, but once it was gone it was gone. Perhaps not all Virgos would respond the same about losing a car, but I guarantee that there are things you could change that would upset them as much as my wife was about her car. Try rearranging the furniture in their favorite room and see what happens.

One of our Virgo friends related to me how much she hates change. She told me of two examples. She just started a new job and this has caused her to change her routine, which caused her an enormous amount of stress which she was still going through. The second example was that she had been taking care of her ill mother for a long time. On a daily basis, she worked, went to see her mother in a care facility, as well as taking care of her own life. This may sound like a lot, but that wasn't what bothered her. What threw her world into turmoil was when her mother died. It wasn't that she loved her mother so much, which she did, but the change in schedule is what truly upset her. She had become accustomed to her hectic lifestyle, and changing it really caused her upset. Change for a Virgo is more upsetting than it would be to the rest of us. If change upsets you (and you'd be unique if it didn't), then multiply that upset by at least three and you may have just a slight inkling of how change affects your favorite Virgo.

Last year for my wife's birthday, I bought her a new, modern, two-line, cordless phone with a headset to try and make her life easier. I thought it would be a great idea to hook it up for her while she was gone and surprise her. I was the one who was in for a surprise. Her first reaction was absolute horror! She wanted to know how I could change the heart of her business during such a busy time with her coordinating the Fog Fest and expect her to get accustomed to it. I was told, in no uncertain terms, that she just could not deal with the change. She said that it was akin to giving a surgeon a new, untested scalpel right in the middle of open-heart surgery. After we had some heated words about it (I was upset that she was so upset and didn't even appreciate my gift), the new phone was removed and replaced with her old, funky phone that doesn't even hang up half of the time. I was shocked and hurt that she hated my gift. I thought I was being so thoughtful, and instead I discovered that I had upset her on her birthday. The old phone was still in use months later. She said that in January, when her business is slower, she would try it again. It still caused her considerable upset. As a matter of fact, she requested that I hook it up to a single phone line that was going to be put in for her Fog Fest office; however, it is a two-line phone and she still wouldn't use the headset because she said it wasn't what she thought it would be. She apparently wanted to wait until a Virgo invented a cordless headset with dialing so easy you just have to think about it and it will call the number you had in mind! Finally, almost a year after I bought the phone, we hooked it up and she is using it. She is actually using it on a regular basis and finds it very convenient; however, she has found several things that don't please her about it. It could be the most advanced phone on the planet today and she would still find something that could be improved.

Which brings me to my wife's computer. You would think that someone whose livelihood is dependent upon computers would want to have the most modern computer available. You would be wrong regarding my wife. After years of her using an IBM 386, I finally talked her into upgrading to a 486. Years later, after the world had moved on to Pentiums, I was able to convince her that she should upgrade again. Sounds like she adjusted to change pretty easily, doesn't it? Well, she didn't. Although she now has a Pentium, she continues to use the keyboard from the 386. Not only that, but she doesn't like the way some upgraded programs operate. It doesn't matter to her that they operate faster or more efficiently because they are different and she feels that she loses valuable time relearning how to use them. I don't know if I will ever be able to wrestle the old keyboard out of her hands until it just stops working. When it does stop working, she will look frantically for a replacement for it that is exactly alike. Never mind that they don't make them any more, because she doesn't want to change. She types totally by touch, even the function keys. She says, "You wouldn't give Beethoven a new keyboard and expect him to still play his masterpieces, would you?" (Actually, I would!) I, on the other hand, have used a plethora of computers and keyboards and have adjusted to the changes just fine. Sure, I made a few mistakes, and granted I don't type by touch, but I get used to the new systems and keyboards. I admit that I am a more computer savvy person than she is, but I don't think it would matter if she was a computer whiz, she would still want her old keyboard. Change is more upsetting to a Virgo than it is to the rest of us (anal-retentive not withstanding).

I don't want to make it sound like we never buy anything new, because we do, but many of the things we acquire cause upsets until my wife has become accustomed to the changes. I am fond of state-of-the-art electronic equipment. Over the last two years, I have bought a new big-screen TV and surround-sound audio system. It is a wonderful system with great sound and picture. I love it. My wife, however, hates when I change things and she can't get used to the remotes. She has told me, on several occasions that if I die before her, she will sell all of the hi-tech stuff and just get a normal television that she can just turn off and on. It isn't that she doesn't enjoy watching our system, but just that it is different from what she has been used to and she doesn't want to learn all over again. She will call me at work to ask me how to make the television operate when I have left it in some mode that she doesn't know. When she calls, you would think someone had just died, because she gets so upset.

Rule Number Ten: <u>Change causes upset.</u>

The important thing to remember is that it isn't personal; it is just how a Virgo is.

Chapter 11

PUTTING IT ALL TOGETHER

What is it that we have learned about Virgos that can help us to have a fuller, more meaningful existence with them?

<u>One</u>. ***The Virgo is perfect.*** If you don't believe me, just ask one. The truth is we are all perfect just how we are. Only the Virgo is acutely aware of this fact.

<u>Two</u>. ***Never ask a Virgo to prove themself after they have done exceptional work.*** This may also be something that no one likes, but the Virgo will find it especially heinous. It goes against Rule One.

<u>Three</u>. ***Virgos love confirmation of their perfection.*** Still don't believe me? You can test it in two ways. First, never compliment your Virgo on a job well done or admit that they did it better than you. You'll find out the hard way how right I am. Second, compliment them on a job well done and watch them glow. Sure, we all love to be complimented, but the Virgo craves it! They need it! They wait for it! And besides, it is easier to deal with than the first method.

<u>Four</u>. ***Don't make mistakes.*** If you really don't want to have to listen to them point out the errors of your ways, then just avoid mistakes. That should be simple, right? Well, maybe not. That is why we should always be willing to admit our mistakes to a Virgo. They don't expect ***us*** to be perfect, but they do expect us to ***admit*** we aren't. After all, how could we be? We're not Virgos.

<u>Five</u>. ***Virgos like things nice and tidy.*** It would be nice to think that we all like that, but let's admit it—some of us just don't care. But if you want a peaceful existence with your Virgo, then pick it up and put it where it belongs.

<u>Six</u>. ***Don't fight it, just do it.*** You've tried to fight with them about it and what did that lead to? Nothing pleasant, I assure you. When a

Virgo wants something done, they cannot move forward until they know it is accomplished.

<u>Seven</u>. ***Survival is dependent on our being able to adapt to the Virgo environment.*** You can resist it if you want, but then why buy a book about how to survive living with a Virgo if you are going to ignore this very important premise?

<u>Eight</u>. ***Virgos love organization.*** Once again you may find yourself saying, "But I like things organized, too." Perhaps you do, but would you lose sleep over something being out of place? Many a Virgo will. Don't believe me? Try moving things around sometime without their knowledge and see what you get.

<u>Nine</u>. ***Don't get mad, get used to it.*** It is hard to get anyone to change their ways. I will be the first to admit that I will drag my feet if someone wants me to change something about myself. As a matter of fact, I could get downright ornery. But it's a heck of a lot easier to try to adjust to the environment I am in than to try to change the environment. This is especially true with trying to change a Virgo. You will be a lot happier if you just do whatever it is that your Virgo requests than to fight it. You will expend far less time and energy.

<u>Ten</u>. ***Change causes upset.*** Once again, this is something that affects everyone, but no one as much as the Virgo. When I learned this premise in the *est* training years ago, it was something that I felt was extremely useful in dealing with life's ups and downs. When I married a Virgo, I discovered how absolutely on target it was. Your Virgo hates change. I guarantee it. Just ask them.

Try to understand what makes your Virgo tick and you will create a much more peaceful and happy universe for yourself. With all the turmoil in the world today, we all need to eliminate as much friction as we possibly can. This book was designed to help you accomplish that. If my theory proves to be right that there are more Virgos around us than any of us were aware of and you use this book to get along with those Virgos better, then the world is bound to be a better place. Now that can't be all bad, can it?